A
Rookie
reader®

In My
Backyard

Written by Don L. Curry
Illustrated by Erin O'Leary Brown

Children's Press®
A Division of Scholastic Inc.
New York • Toronto • London • Auckland • Sydney
Mexico City • New Delhi • Hong Kong
Danbury, Connecticut

To Catlin Elementary School in Kelso, Washington—thank you
for taking such good care of the kid I was.
—D.L.C.

To my mother, Shelley, who has always created a beautiful backyard.
—E.O.B.

Reading Consultants

Linda Cornwell
Literacy Specialist

Katharine A. Kane
Education Consultant
(Retired, San Diego County Office of Education
and San Diego State University)

Library of Congress Cataloging-in-Publication Data
Curry, Don L.
  In my backyard / written by Don L. Curry;
illustrated by Erin O'Leary Brown.
      p. cm. — (A rookie reader)
  Summary: A girl sees many signs of spring in her backyard,
including a frog and a bird.
  ISBN 0-516-25898-2 (lib. bdg.)   0-516-26825-2 (pbk.)
  [1. Spring—Fiction.] I. O'Leary Brown, Erin, ill. II. Title. III. Series.
  PZ7.C93595In 2003
  [E]–dc21
                                        2003007112

CHILDREN'S PRESS, and A ROOKIE READER®, and associated logos are trademarks
and or registered trademarks of Scholastic Library Publishing. SCHOLASTIC and
associated logos are trademarks and or registered trademarks of Scholastic Inc.
1 2 3 4 5 6 7 8 9 10 R 13 12 11 10 09 08 07 06 05 04

Trees have buds in my backyard.

Frogs have mud in my backyard.

Ants have hills in my backyard.

Birds have nests in my backyard.

9

Seeds have water in my backyard.

Ladybugs have flowers
in my backyard.

Flowers have sunshine
in my backyard.

Squirrels have fun in my backyard.

Spiders have webs in my backyard.

Ducks have ducklings
in my backyard.

It is spring in my backyard.

Word List (26 words)

ants	frogs	ladybugs	squirrels
backyard	fun	mud	sunshine
birds	have	my	trees
buds	hills	nests	water
ducklings	in	seeds	webs
ducks	is	spiders	
flowers	it	spring	

About the Author

Don L. Curry is a writer, editor, and educational consultant who lives and works in New York City. When he is not writing or speaking to groups of children or teachers, Don can generally be found in Central Park reading or riding his bike exploring the streets of the greatest city on Earth.

About the Illustrator

Erin O'Leary Brown gets lots of ideas and inspiration for her artwork from her own backyard in upstate New York. When spring brings warm weather, she loves to tuck her sketchbook under her arm and head outside in search of little creatures and interesting details of nature to draw. When she is not painting or drawing, she enjoys spending time with her husband, Craig, their two dogs, Sawyer and Sendak, and their cat, Kitty.